STEP
-BY-
STEP
DECLUTTERING

LETTING GO OF THE EXCESS SO YOU HAVE
ROOM FOR WHAT MATTERS MOST

SARAH MUELLER

Copyright 2021 Sarah Mueller. All rights reserved.
Cover Design by Sarah Mueller

ISBN 978-1-7365859-0-0

Disclosure
This book contains affiliate links. This means that when you make a purchase
at a site via a link I have provided, I make a small commission at no additional cost to you.
I am disclosing this in accordance with the Federal Trade Commission's 16 CFR, Part 255:
"Guides Concerning the Use of Endorsements and Testimonials in Advertising."
Regardless of whether or not I receive a commission, I only recommend products that I
personally use and genuinely recommend, and I always have my readers' best interest at
heart. Thank you so much for supporting this book in this way!

Table of Contents

Digital Add-ons
Page 4

Introduction
How I Started Decluttering - Page 5

Section 1
Gaining the Decluttering Mindset - Page 6

Section 2
Quick Wins Build Confidence - Page 23

Section 3
Start with the Kitchen - Page 33

Section 4
Build Momentum - Page 46

Section 5
You're Becoming a Pro! - Page 56

Conclusion
Page 64

The Decluttering School Roadmap
Page 65

About the Author
Page 66

Worksheets

Digital Add-ons

If you didn't yet order the complete digital Step-by-Step Decluttering Workshop, you can order it by going to this link:

https://declutteringschool.com/shop/

You'll get the ebook + audiobook versions of Step-by-Step Decluttering PLUS helpful video training and a 30 day email challenge.

30 Day Decluttering Challenge

Once you've purchased the digital workshop, stay organized! It's easy for you to keep track of your login to our Decluttering School website by noting your username and password below.

Username:

Password:

Log in to your account here: members.declutteringschool.com

Questions about your order? Email us at sarah@declutteringschool.com

Introduction

I started decluttering when I looked around our home and realized that much of our hard earned money was buying things that we weren't using. We were paying good money for things that gathered dust! Toys, furniture, kitchen tools, baskets and bins, tools. So much of it sat idle causing more mess than the enjoyment I expected.

So I looked for ways to better organize. I rearranged and tried to come up with strategies to better use our possessions. I devised toy rotation systems. I purchased more storage solutions. But the problem was still there.

It was about this time that the minimalist movement was picking up steam. I started reading. I got hooked to the idea that we didn't need all this "stuff." Less is more! It was an awesome feeling, and I became a true convert.
Honestly, I got a little carried away.

That was quite a while ago. Now I'm more reasonable with my possessions and my distaste for clutter. I understand that not everyone feels the same way about clutter that I do. But I do love to help people experience the freedom that comes from decluttering. I love to help them discover what it's like to let go of all that stuff that's dragging them down.

So I decided to write this book.

Section 1
Gaining the Decluttering Mindset

On my blog, Decluttering School, I write a lot about decluttering. And the number one issue that people mention repeatedly is how to get started. Facing a cluttered house, whether a little or a lot, is a daunting task and it's easy to feel defeated and give up. After all, the clutter just regenerates itself, doesn't it?

Not necessarily.

In this book, I'm going to teach you a decluttering strategy that will help you get started, stay on track and see real, lasting progress. If you stick to the steps in this book, you'll gain an understanding of how your house became cluttered in the first place and how to fix the problem. You may even grow to enjoy decluttering (like I do!). Even if you don't end up loving the process, I know you'll love the end result – a neater, more pleasant home with enough room for your family to live your lives.

Ground rules for this book

In doing the research and interviews for this book, I was reminded over and over again that decluttering is a very emotional process. It's not just about getting rid of a few things. It's about making difficult decisions related to important things in our lives. If it were easy, you'd be done by now and you wouldn't feel such angst over the whole process.

So I thought it would be helpful to set some ground rules before we get started. If you're a reader of my blog, you know that I'm all about encouragement to do the hard things in life, but also that we should all give ourselves grace. By this I mean we should be kind to ourselves and not set unreasonable expectations on our own shoulders.

So here are your decluttering rules:

1 — **I will not compare myself to other people,** whether they're more or less cluttered than me, unless it's for positive inspiration.

2 — **I will not engage in negative self-talk.** When I'm tempted to do this, I'll remind myself that negativity isn't helpful and I'm making progress, even if it's slow.

3 — **I will not apologize for what I do and don't love.** I don't need to justify why I love something (and want to keep it) or why I don't love something and want to declutter it.

4 — **I won't allow other people to guilt me** into doing something I don't want to do, whether it's keeping something or getting rid of something.

5 — **I won't declutter other people's things** without their permission (except children – we'll get to that later).

6 — **I will take it as slowly as I need to,** taking my personal responsibilities and limitations into account. (Remember, no negative self-talk!)

7 — **I will celebrate my progress!**

8 — **I understand not everyone is as excited** about this process as I am, but that doesn't mean I shouldn't keep going.

9 — **I will remember that decluttering can be** a difficult, emotional process. I'll keep that in mind when I'm feeling discouraged.

Sound good? Excellent. I'm going to hold you to them!

If you can keep these rules in mind, you'll have a much more successful decluttering experience. Come back to this page if you need a pep talk later on.

My job in this book

There's one more thing I need to tell you. These rules apply to *my* advice, too. I do not want to pressure you into specific decisions. It doesn't matter what I think about your possessions. It's not my job to tell you what to get rid of and what to keep. My job is to help you learn and apply a framework for making those decisions on your own. In this book, I *do* include my own personal thoughts on things I've decluttered. I may push you a bit out of your comfort zone. But the decision is still yours. So don't let anyone else make it for you, not even me.

What is clutter?

Clutter is a very negative-sounding word. It sounds messy, untidy, like a bunch of junk. No one likes to admit they have lots of clutter!

Here are a few definitions of clutter:

Erin Doland of Unclutterer says, *"Clutter is any distraction that gets in the way of a remarkable life."*

Joshua Becker of Becoming Minimalist says that, *"clutter is too much stuff in too small a space."*

William Morris's famous quote about clutter is, *"Have nothing in your house that you do not know to be useful or believe to be beautiful."*

According to Marie Kondo, clutter is anything that does not spark joy.

So it seems like what is clutter is a very personal question. One man's trash is another man's treasure (and vice versa!).

So for the purposes of this book, I'll use the word *clutter* to refer to anything that you have but don't want to keep. It may or may not have any actual monetary value. It may be little random things in your junk drawer or great big pieces of furniture! It may be expensive, heirloom items or things from the dollar store.

Clutter:
Anything in your possession
that you don't want to keep

Clutter can, in fact, be very nicely organized. If you don't want it or love it, then it's still clutter. **The key here is the word "you." You** get to decide what is clutter in **your** home.

Remember Ground Rule 3?

I will not apologize for what I do and don't love.
I don't want you to feel you have to conform to someone else's idea of what is clutter and what is not. This should take a lot of the pressure off to get rid of a set amount of stuff or have a perfectly minimalist result when you're done.

So to keep it simple, I'll refer to all that unwanted stuff as just clutter. You'll understand that **you** get to define what that means for you.

A caution about the worksheets in this book

This book contains several worksheets. You may feel that some of them are silly or overly obvious. Do you really need to take the time to complete all of them? Maybe you'll be tempted to just read them and answer the questions in your head.

Please don't do this.

You bought this book for a reason. You've got some quantity of clutter and you haven't been able to get rid of it. These worksheets will help you gain meaningful insight on how you got to this place and how to move forward. The physical act of filling them in will have a real impact on your success!

So please, humor me and make sure to do your homework along the way. You'll see how it all comes together at the end.

The cost of clutter

Do you realize how much clutter is truly costing you and weighing you down?

Living with clutter is a little bit like the old story of the frog in the pot. Little by little, the heat is turned up and the frog never notices he's being cooked until it's too late. With clutter, at first you don't notice it's there, until one day you look around and suddenly realize you're swamped!

So we've already established that you're not satisfied with the amount of clutter in your home. That's why you bought this book. But let's take some time to talk about the price that clutter is costing you. The more you understand this, the more motivated you'll be to do something about the problem. After all, if there's no problem, there's no reason to make a change.

Here are some of the effects of clutter:

- Clutter causes frustration.
- Clutter causes more time spent looking for things.
- You may end up replacing things that get lost in the clutter, costing more money.
- Clutter is depressing.
- Clutter causes embarrassment.
- Clutter costs extra money to move.
- Clutter may require that you need a bigger house (and a bigger mortgage) than you'd otherwise require.
- Hanging on to clutter causes you to miss opportunities to bless other people with your excess.
- Hanging on to clutter points you toward the past so that you miss out on the present and possibilities for the future.
- Clutter represents wasted money.
- Clutter collects dust.
- Clutter may cause arguments.
- Clutter is visually unappealing.
- Children can become over-stimulated in a cluttered room, causing behavior problems.
- Hanging on to clutter may represent a negative mindset that's holding you back from the new experiences and opportunities.
- Clutter can be dangerous! Think about trip hazards and, in extreme cases, fire hazards.
- Clutter causes more housework.
- Cluttered spaces make it hard to motivate yourself to start projects. Cooking in an uncluttered kitchen is more pleasant than cooking in a messy, cluttered one.
- Clutter can cause unresolved guilt over unused purchases or things you should be cleaning up.
- Clutter hides the things you love.
- Clutter may even cost you actual dollars if you have a storage unit like one in ten Americans, according to the *New York Times*.

Accumulated clutter

If your clutter has accumulated over time, you may not even realize the burden it's putting on you. It may be like a nagging voice in the back of your head that you manage to ignore most of the time. Imagine if that voice wasn't there anymore! All the guilt and frustration would be gone, too.

It's time to let it go.

Now that we've indulged a bit in some negativity, let's turn to the brighter side: the side that's waiting for you!

What are the benefits of a decluttered home?

- Decluttered spaces allow the treasures to be enjoyed.
- Decluttered spaces are pleasant and enjoyable to be in.
- Decluttered spaces are easy to keep clean and are enjoyable to work and play in.
- In a decluttered space, you can find what you're looking for.
- It's easier to focus on your work and your family in a decluttered space.
- You'll have more time for your priorities in a decluttered space.
- In a decluttered space you'll be less tempted to buy unnecessary things and destroy your hard work.
- You'll find yourself investing in quality purchases (clothing, furniture, etc.) which will last much longer in a decluttered home. There's much more incentive to be thoughtful when purchasing and to focus on the long run.
- Decluttered spaces have more room to work and play.
- Decluttered spaces teach children good habits for the future.
- Kids will play more peacefully and for longer periods in a decluttered home with fewer toys.
- Decluttered homes point towards the future instead of hanging on to the past.

ACTION ITEM

Look at the "*Clutter: Cost / Benefit*" worksheet and check off the costs and benefits that apply to you.

What are your issues? Goals? Vision?

Before you start any large project, it's sensible to do a little upfront planning. If we view decluttering as a journey, then you need to identify where you are so you can figure out how to get where you want to go. We'll start actually decluttering shortly. But first, I want you to think about where you are right now.

ACTION ITEM

Fill out the "*You Are Here*" worksheet to help you prepare to set off on your journey.

A quick dose of realism

Ok – before the sappiness gets too deep, let's take a quick check point, shall we? Of course, you know I'm not saying you'll never have to clean up again. I'm not saying your home will be zen-like and your rooms will always be tidy. Decluttering isn't the solution to all life's problems. Nope – messes will still be made, shoes will still be left lying around and the dishes will still pile up (though not quite as high). So I'm not promising you a perfect home or a perfect life.

But.

But making messes is part of life! Without those shoes and those dishes, it means your home is empty. That's a very sad thing, isn't it? No one wants that. What decluttering *will* do for you is to make it much easier to recover from a mess or do day-to-day upkeep. And you won't experience all those other nasty side effects like guilt and embarrassment, either.

Don't expect perfection, but do expect improvement.

Your Decluttering Toolkit

The most important tool you'll have as you go through the decluttering process is your mindset. We spent a good chunk of time on the cost of clutter and the benefits of decluttering. The purpose of this activity is to help you see the real cost your clutter is putting on you. You will only be motivated to take action when you decide you don't want to bear this burden anymore.

Some people don't mind the clutter. They truly like all the things they're keeping (or perhaps they're not being honest with themselves). This book isn't for them.

So before you start decluttering, I want you to declare that you've had enough! I want you to get fired up about making a change for the better! You have to be passionate about cleaning up and clearing out! You're going to need that energy!

When I was doing research for this book, I kept hearing over and over again:

"How will I stay motivated to declutter?"

"Will there be a clear step-by-step plan outlined?"

"Will I actually be able to follow through with decluttering without getting too frustrated?"

So I've developed a set of tools for you to use as you go through the book and declutter your home. It's going to be about getting motivated and excited about the process, and guiding you through manageable steps with milestones along the way so you don't get discouraged.

Here's our plan:

A series of worksheets.

You've already completed two of them. I don't want you to just start grabbing stuff to throw away. You'll get tired of that awfully quickly! Instead, I want you to take some time upfront to do a little planning and then track your progress as you go.

A Milestones Grid.

You've got a grid with 12 different tasks that will guide you on your decluttering journey. Studies have shown that people who track their progress are more motivated and more likely to finish what they started, according to *Psychology Today*.

So let's track! This simple grid gives you the step-by-step plan of the decluttering activities you'll do. When you finish the grid, you'll have a huge amount of progress under your belt! And we will celebrate!

How to decide what to do with all that stuff.

I know you're probably anxious to get started, and we're almost ready! But first we need to cover one more important question: what to do with all that stuff?

You may be tempted to find exactly the right home for each and everything you declutter. You might have decluttered in the past and ended up with seven (or more!) categories of things you no longer wanted. I want to caution you against this approach.

The more difficult you make it to get rid of your clutter, the less likely you are to do so. You've got to make it EASY to dispose of that clutter! The more clutter you have, the easier it needs to be.

Here are your options:

1. Trash /recycle

Obviously this is the quickest way to get rid of clutter. I know some people are concerned about waste, but isn't it more wasteful to have something consuming space on a shelf or in a cupboard of your home for too long? I'm all about recycling – heck, I even have a compost pile! But when you're decluttering, especially in large quantities, it's more important to have the stuff gone than it is to keep it out of the landfill. If you try to find the perfect home for each item you declutter, you'll be burned out in no time.

So please be prepared to throw some things away (or recycle them if you're dealing with paper).

2. Donate

Lots of clutter can receive a new life by passing it on to a place like a thrift store. You can take most household goods to the thrift store and they'll sort through them and sell what's usable. They'll frequently recycle textiles that are no longer sellable.

I take clutter to the thrift store all the time. I really enjoy this option because I know how glad people are to find useful things at thrift store prices. It's a great way to bless someone else with your clutter. It doesn't matter that you don't get to give the gift in person – it's still helping someone out.

You can also drop clothing into those donation bins you may see in the parking lots of shopping centers. This is a great choice when you're short on time and you don't have a thrift store nearby.

Some organizations will even pick up your clutter right at your door! I did this several times when we were preparing to move. It's a wonderful option if you've got lots to donate or you aren't able to do the heavy lifting to get the items to the drop-off location.

The best way to find an organization that picks up donations is to do a Google search for "donation pick up" or to ask around, as they vary by region.

3. Ask your friends

This is another great way to get rid of clutter. This option is best for individual items that are in good condition. Take a quick picture of your item, post it on Facebook and see if anyone wants it. I've done this with larger items including, a toaster oven, a like-new comforter and a big box of homeschool books. I've also been the recipient of many things through this method. But remember, this isn't a great option if you have lots of clutter or if you want to get rid of things quickly.

4. Find a worthy cause

If you have unique or special items that you want to declutter, there are a couple of interesting ways you can get rid of them. For instance, if you have an old high school letterman jacket you might see if the local high school drama department would like to have it. Art and craft supplies can go to a daycare or preschool. Clothing, bedding and baby equipment can also go to women's shelters or homeless shelters. Animal shelters love old towels. Using these options may make you feel much better about getting rid of your clutter.

5. Repurpose

For certain sentimental things, you may choose to get creative and turn them into something new. We'll get into some specifics in a bit. This strategy is best reserved for very special things like wedding gowns, baby items, limited special mementos and perhaps children's artwork. So do keep this option in mind.

If you're not interested in this option, don't give it another thought. Frequently people will hang on to things with the intention of doing something special with them, but they never get around to it. These things just end up being more clutter.

6. Sell

I've saved this option for last because it's usually the most time consuming.

We've all heard about people who had a treasure in their attic and sold it for a million dollars on Antiques Roadshow. But the reason these stories are so compelling is that they're the exception rather than the rule. Most clutter can't be sold for a profit, or it will take quite a bit of time to do so.

Selling tips

However if you do have something you want to sell here are some tips.

Research

1) Do some research to find out what it's worth. A quick search on eBay or even Amazon will help to determine the value of an item. It is surprising what things you can find on eBay!

Social Media

2) If your item is large, you'll probably want to sell it locally. You can use Craigslist or Facebook groups (search "name of your town yard sale" on Facebook) to find buyers for your item. If your item is smaller you may decide to use eBay or Amazon. Just make sure to take shipping costs into account and to put a price on your time so you're not spending hours selling things for pennies. And be safe and meet any buyers in a public location.

What about yard sales?

You may also choose to have a yard sale. Some people are masters at making money from yard sales. I'm not one of them. Usually, it's worth it to have the clutter out the door instead of letting it pile up in anticipation of a yard sale that may or may not make much money. My focus is on helping you declutter, not make money at a yard sale so I'm not going to recommend that to you. However, if you have had success with yard sales in the past and you know you'll make it happen within the next couple weeks, then go for it.

Above all when you're deciding whether or not to sell something, don't put too much emphasis on the price you paid for it. Just like a new car loses value as soon as you drive it off the lot, the same is true with most of the things we buy. You're not going to get back what you paid.

In this list of options, I put a lot of emphasis on giving things away.

Giving away some of your more "useful" clutter is a great idea for a couple reasons:

- You will bless someone else with something you don't need or want.

- When you sell something, you may be frustrated that you didn't get enough money for that item. But when you give something away, you stop focusing on whether you got enough for it. It saves you a lot of inconvenience and frustration, especially if you felt like you paid a lot for that item.

- It's much quicker to give things away, especially in large loads, than it is to sell them, repurpose them, or find homes for them one by one.

- Giving gifts is fun! Trying to sell clutter is usually not as much fun.

ACTION ITEM

Complete the "*What To Do With All That Stuff*" worksheet.

NOTES:

Section 2
Quick Wins Build Confidence

Easy setup and a decluttering framework

Now that you've done your homework, we get to the nitty gritty of decluttering. Whenever you declutter, you'll need to grab a few things:

- [ ] 1 - 3 laundry baskets or large boxes
- [ ] large trash bag (heavy duty black is preferable)
- [ ] timer (it's easy to use the one on your phone)
- [ ] notepad or piece of paper and a pencil

In addition, you'll need a clear space to work – a table, a counter, a clear area of floor or even on top of a bed are all good options. Decide what you'll do with the clutter you're disposing of (donations, give to friends, sell, etc.) Refer back to the "Donate / Sell / Trash" worksheet if necessary. Label your baskets accordingly with sticky notes.

The basic decluttering framework

- [ ] Identify what area to declutter
- [ ] Set the timer
- [ ] Collect your items (2 minutes)
- [ ] Sort / take notes (8 minutes)
- [ ] Dispose of the clutter (5 minutes)
- [ ] Clean everything up (5 minutes)

Decluttering framework:

Identify what you're going to work on.

Is it a drawer, a cupboard, an entire room? You absolutely can and should work on small areas at a time, especially at the beginning. Decide what you're going to do with the things you declutter (you can refer back to the worksheet if necessary). This will help you decide how to sort things.

Set the timer for 20 minutes.

The timer will be more useful than you realize. The timer will keep you focused (and honest!). You may even end up having a few false starts if you get distracted during one of the early steps. If you run out of time during any step, determine if you have another 20 minutes to keep going or if you need to come back and re-start later. Maybe the area you picked was too big or the items too sentimental. Timers are especially motivating for people with ADHD. So let your timer help keep you on track.

There's no need to re-set the timer for each step of this process, but you'll notice that each step needs to be brief. The idea here is to work quickly and make quick decisions.

Collect the things you're decluttering.

Bring them to your work area. If there's a lot to work through, do it in stages. Empty drawers and cupboards. Get the things out where you can look at them.

Sort.

Take each item in turn and ask yourself: Is this useful? Do I like it? Do I have room to keep it? Do I already have something similar that I like more? Do I want to keep it? Am I still using this item?

Dispose of.

If the answer to any of these questions is no, you've identified clutter. Decide which of your baskets it belongs in (donate, give to a friend, etc.). If it's trash, put it in the trash bag. As you go, jot down any relevant notes (for example, "post the toaster oven on Facebook," or "ask Jen if she wants that red sweater.") Take pictures right away with your phone if you need to. Also jot down notes of things you'd like to buy to help organize your space later on.

Clean up.

Put back the things that you're keeping. Hopefully you've got a lot less to put back now! Take out the trash. Put a load of things in your car for the thrift store and pick a time to drop them off. Text your friends or post on Facebook about any items you're giving away. In general, remove all the clutter you identified before you continue to another area.

Whew! You made it!

Did you beat the timer? Those 20 minutes seem like a race. And that's intentional. You don't want to agonize over these decisions, especially not at this point. This is a super-quick burst of activity designed to get you moving and familiar with working and completing the process.

These steps may seem obvious. It doesn't sound like rocket science, does it? But many people skip one or more of these steps. How often have you jumped into decluttering without first clearly identifying what area you're working on? This is a recipe for frustration and overwhelm! How many times have you skipped or delayed the clean up? In that case, you're left with a bigger mess than when you started.

So make sure to pick a manageable area and work through all the steps before you start another area.

There's one more question you should ask before you decide if something qualifies as clutter: "Is it mine to declutter?" As you declutter, you'll come across things belonging to other family members. I usually keep those in a separate pile and return them to their owners when I'm done decluttering. If you've got a lot of things in this category, grab a basket to hold them as well.

A side note about the trash bag

Invariably someone will wander by as you're decluttering. If you're using trash bags that aren't the heavy-duty kind, you might get comments like "Oh, but I thought you loved that sweater (that shrunk 3 sizes in the dryer,)" or "Why are you throwing away perfectly good shampoo?" You can avoid this issue completely by using black trash bags. If no one can see what's in the bag, you'll prevent lots of questions and problems. Of course, you're not decluttering things that belong to other people, so you have every right to discard something of your own.

This setup works whether you're spending 20 minutes decluttering or 5 hours (although I don't recommend 5 hours – that's probably much too long of a stretch).

Your first 20-minute decluttering session

Now that you've got the decluttering framework down, it's time to take it for a test drive. Pick a very small area of your home, even just a shelf or a drawer, to work on. Keep it focused! Pick an area with things that you're not overly attached to. You want to get some easy wins down before you tackle harder items.

It's so critical to tackle easier items first because:

- *you'll make decisions more quickly*
- *you won't get bogged down on a trip through memory lane*
- *you'll have an easier time letting go of more things*

ACTION ITEM

Grab your baskets or boxes. Set a timer for 20 minutes. Work through your chosen area using the decluttering framework. Make sure to finish cleaning up when you're done. Check off the box on your "*Milestones Grid*."

Then **CELEBRATE**!

Do it again

If your first 20-minute decluttering session was a big success or if you like or need to work in short bursts, do a few more of these. Just pick another very focused area and go through the process. These quick sessions are great for parents with tiny children. This is also a great technique for people who have physical limitations which prevent them from working for long periods. Just make sure to set the timer and go through the whole process all the way to the end.

Even if you do just 20 minutes of decluttering every day for a month, you'll be amazed at the progress you will see at the end.

Resistant family members

Do you have someone in your life or even your home who is going to interfere with your decluttering efforts?

Sometimes, I think if I could just do exactly what *I* want, my life would be perfectly decluttered. It's those pesky family members who get in the way. Of course, this isn't true, but decluttering, like any kind of change, requires communication with the people in your life. And not everyone wants the same things you do.

Here are the kinds of issues people run into:

Someone keeps bringing in clutter.

Whether it's children or other adults, some people just seem to collect the clutter. It doesn't bother them in the least that they're frustrating your efforts. They fill up the shelves and refuse to pick up their things or participate in house-cleaning efforts.

Someone else pours on the guilt.

Some people want to save all kinds of things AND they think you should feel the same way. They may not have room for some family heirloom or "useful" item, but they think that you should store it "just in case." They are appalled that you'd get rid of perfectly useful items and they don't hesitate to remind you how wasteful that is.

Someone keeps giving your children more clutter.

Some relatives just can't help themselves. They love to spoil your kids with gifts or clothing and they have no regard for your protests.

I wish I had magic answers for these problems. The solutions usually boil down to two things: communication and putting your foot down.

Remember Ground Rules 4, 5 and 8. Here they are again:

4 **I won't allow other people to guilt me**
into doing something I don't want to do, whether it's keeping something or getting rid of something.

5 **I won't declutter other people's things**
without their permission (except children – we'll get to that later).

8 **I understand not everyone is as excited**
about this process as I am, but that doesn't mean I shouldn't keep going.

Communication

If you have someone in your life who's actively interfering with your decluttering efforts, the first step to take is communication. Try to understand where they are coming from. Did they grow up in a very frugal family where they had to scrimp and save every penny? Maybe that's why they can't let go of things. Is giving gifts to your children their favorite way of showing love? Are they hanging on to some element of the past (remember the *"Cost of Clutter"* worksheet)? Do they not know how to properly clean up? Do they need a better system to organize their belongings?

Multiple generations

I heard from several families living with multiple generations under one roof. I don't have much personal experience with this, so I can only imagine that these situations require on-going and intense communication to help everyone be comfortable and satisfied. Focus on working together on solutions.

The "Why"

Once you have thought a bit about WHY they're so resistant, you can work on the issue. Help them to see that you truly want to understand their motives. Don't try to change them, but do see if you can offer suggestions. If someone else is struggling with clutter, they might welcome some constructive suggestions as long as they know you're not trying to "fix" them.

Working together

If you're working together on an issue, do try to keep the scope small and focused. Don't say, "The kitchen is a disaster!" Instead, say, "Let's see if we can organize this pantry so that cooking is easier." Don't say, "You leave your stuff all over the place!" This may be true, but it's not productive. Instead, say, "I bought some hooks for our coats. Where do you think we should hang them?" or, "What can we do to keep these shoes neater?"

Perhaps your resistant peeps would welcome help with decluttering and cleaning up! They weren't born neatniks anymore than you were. So find ways to work with them to find solutions to your problems. Teach kids good habits (clear up your dishes, dear) and let them see you decluttering. Work with them on decluttering an area of their choice.

Eventually, you may find that your efforts fall on deaf ears. That's when it's time to put your foot down.

This approach works best with children and adults who don't live in your home. (For adults living with you, you'll probably have to do more communicating than insisting.)

You decide what your standards are and then you communicate and enforce them. *Here are some examples:*

- Kids' bedrooms must be picked up by ____ or they lose screen time (or their phone) for the day. Don't give reminders – just make your statement and enforce when needed. You'll probably only have to do this once or twice before the message sinks in and the room stays neat.

- Put any toys that aren't picked up in timeout for several days. If they're left out repeatedly, declutter them out of the house.

- Give kids a box for craft supplies. They can keep whatever fits in the box. Everything else will be decluttered.

- Give your husband (and perhaps each family member) a box for mail and papers. That person is responsible for his or her own box.

- Notify your family that you don't have room to store a certain item any more. If anyone wants it, you'll be happy to get it to them; otherwise, it's scheduled for donation in two weeks.

Unwanted gifts

You may feel free to donate them after the gift giver has gone home. If you're questioned about this later, smile, take a deep breath, and say you didn't have room to keep them or the gifts weren't a good fit for your children. Then change the subject.

It's possible, although perhaps difficult, to do all of these things with a gentle voice and a smile on your face. Putting your foot down doesn't have to involve raising your voice. Decide what you want and then figure out how to get it.

These steps aren't about being mean. They're about setting boundaries with the people you love. Kids need to learn personal responsibility. The more you maintain these boundaries and limits, the easier it gets. Plus, the people in your life will see that you mean business and they'll stop giving you such a hard time.

Hopefully, you won't need to put these elements into practice just yet, but if you do, at least you'll be prepared with some ideas.

What if you love everything?

Some people are able to go through an area, but the pile they end up with is no smaller than when they began. They love everything!

A lot of these cases involve deeply sentimental items (think your wedding gown) and so we'll leave those types of things for Section 5. But if you're feeling this way with practically everything you attempt to declutter, try this.

Go back to why you want to declutter. Do you simply have too much stuff? Are you moving and need to downsize? Do you love the *idea* of your things but you're not happy with the way they're stored or the quantities?

Remember your goals. Remember the cost clutter is putting on you. You cannot be free of the weight of the clutter if you refuse to let any of it go. It gets easier with practice – I promise!

You may have to make some hard choices. Tell yourself you'll pick your three favorites in a category and the rest will be decluttered. This kind of heart wrenching decluttering is like pulling off a bandage – get it over with and the quicker the better. The pain subsides quickly. Often the anticipation is worse than the actual act.

Look for the purpose of things.

Marie Kondo, in The Life-Changing Magic of Tidying Up, reminds us that everything you own has an intended purpose in your life. Once that purpose is fulfilled, you may not need that item anymore. If the purpose isn't fulfilled, maybe it's no longer valid for you. Either way, if an item no longer has a purpose in your home, let it go!

Save the hardest things for last. In Section 5 you'll get a suggested decluttering order, but know that anything that you have an extra sentimental attachment to should be saved for later. It's much easier to declutter dried-up cosmetics or expired food than it is mementos.

Section 3
Start with the Kitchen

Why organizing and decluttering go hand in hand

You can organize without decluttering. In fact, plenty of people call it decluttering when they're mostly just reorganizing and rearranging.

But when you truly declutter, it's much easier to organize what's left. While this isn't a book on organizing, it would be silly of me not to talk about organizing at all. So let's take a short detour into some kitchen organization principles.

Here are *7 **organizing principles*** I use in the kitchen. You can extend most of these principles throughout your house.

It always interests me how other people organize their kitchens. A well organized kitchen employs certain principles. Organized people instinctively use these principles, but if you're not one of those people, you may struggle with how you should organize your own kitchen.

Here are some guidelines to work with as you organize (or re-organize) your kitchen.

Use these 7 simple principles to organize your kitchen:

1. Group small items.

If you do nothing else to organize your kitchen, spend some time "containerizing." This step gives you the biggest bang for your buck.

When you group things like this for storage and display, you gain instant clutter control and a pulled-together look. Instead of a bunch of clutter, a tray or basket unifies the items.

Your brain sees a grouping instead of several random objects.

Most people have a crock next to the stove for cooking spoons and spatulas. This is the same "containerizing" principle at work. Get matching utensils to help this area look less cluttered.

Here are some ideas for groupings:

- a tray with coffee supplies

- a baking basket with cupcake papers, chocolate chips, baking powder and soda, sprinkles, and vanilla extract

- a basket with bags of dried pastas

- a basket full of spice jars – easy to clean and easy to find what you want

- a bin full of lunchbox containers

You can even use baskets that are quite large as long as what you put inside is also fairly large. For example, large bulk bags and containers of oats, rice and flour can go into large bins.

Little bottles and containers should be kept in somewhat smaller baskets, or they'll get lost and you'll end up digging around to find things. But these things are even better stored in glass.

2. Use glass containers to store food.

Food becomes décor when you put it into a pretty glass jar! I've got three glass jars on display in our hutch. Dry goods take up lots of room in the cupboards. Why not put them on display instead?

If you keep a lot of dried goods, they can end up looking quite messy, even if you put the bags into bins or baskets. Instead, remove the packaging and store them in jars. Instant update!

3. Use matching rectangular storage containers.

If you want your cupboards and fridge to look neat and tidy, opt for matching rectangular containers. Containers like this are perfect for leftovers, cookies, cupcakes and muffins.

Glass does require more cupboard space since it won't nest, but it lasts forever, and you avoid storing your food in plastic.

Rectangular containers are easily lined up and you can see at a glance what's inside and how much is left. No more mystery leftovers in the back of the fridge.

4. Keep counters clear.

Counter space should be workspace, not storage. Cooking with cluttered counters is stressful.

Keep your counters as clear as possible, even if it means using wall space or moving some appliances to less convenient storage places. Maybe the stand mixer can be kept on a shelf in the garage?

It probably takes 30 seconds to retrieve a gadget from another part of the house. Don't be afraid to set up a shelf somewhere with kitchen appliances if space is tight in the kitchen.

5. Nest and stack.

Platters, serving bowls and mixing bowls take up tons of room unless you can stack them. I'd even go so far as to declutter a bunch of mismatched mixing bowls in favor of one set that nests perfectly. #perfectionist

All your mixing bowls should be able to stack. The same goes for any frying pans. You'll save tons of space. Plus, your shelves and cupboards will look much neater.

6. Divide your drawers.

Drawer organizers instantly improve the look of shallow drawers for things like utensils, measuring cups and small tools. You can find drawer organizers to fit any drawer or DIY your own.

7. Use labels.

It may be clear to you how things are organized, but without labels, the rest of your family may not understand your system. Labels help everyone put things away where they belong.

This doesn't mean your kitchen doesn't get messed up!

Ha! As if, right? But it does mean that it's easier to clean up, and even when it's messy, you'll still enjoy it.

Organizing the kitchen makes a big difference in how efficient and attractive your kitchen is.

Once again, 7 simple principles to organize your kitchen:

- Group small items into bins or baskets, or onto trays.
- Use glass containers to store food.
- Use matching rectangular storage containers.
- Keep counters clear.
- Nest and stack.
- Divide your drawers.
- Use labels.

What to declutter first

A few years ago, I threw out a non-stick skillet that was terribly scratched up. Even though I hated to cook with it, and I knew that scratched Teflon is a health hazard, my frugal self hesitated. Did I *really* need a new one? But once I tossed it in the trash, it was a huge relief, and I enjoyed my new pans so much more.

So it goes with much of our kitchen clutter. We don't like it and it irritates us to have to use it. We complain that the kitchen is too small. But still, we resist doing something about it. However, once you do take that step, you'll be so happy with your decision. You may even wonder why you waited so long to declutter!

At this point, you've completed one 20-minute decluttering session or maybe several. You've practiced the framework. You are on a roll!

It's time to tackle the kitchen. Why tackle the kitchen? There are a couple reasons.

You've got to start some place. So I picked the kitchen. But it isn't a random choice.

Here's why the kitchen is a great place to start decluttering:

- A decluttered kitchen will save you tons of time. Going back to all the benefits of a decluttered home, a kitchen without excess clutter is a wonderful thing!

- The kitchen tends to accumulate clutter quickly (can I get an amen?) - daily, if your house is like mine. So your initial efforts will have a great payoff. If you were to pick a less public area – maybe your closet - you wouldn't enjoy the rewards of your work nearly as much simply because you spend much less time in the closet than you do in the kitchen.

- A decluttered kitchen will motivate you to keep going in other areas of your home. You might even inspire the rest of the family!

But your kitchen will probably take longer than 20 minutes

(did you just choke on your coffee?) - probably a lot longer. So here's how we'll break it down:

1. Pantry

2. Pots and pans

3. Junk drawer

4. Cleaning supplies and kitchen linens

5. Food storage containers

6. Serving dishes

7. Dishes and cutlery

8. Small appliances

9. Gadgets and tools

10. Paperwork

11. Fridge / freezer

12. Other items

ACTION ITEM

Fill out the *"Kitchen Decluttering"* worksheet to help you make an action plan.

Once you've got your *"Kitchen Decluttering"* worksheet complete, you're ready to start. Are you going to work in 20-minute sessions, or do you have more time? Pick your time and schedule things so you'll have minimum distractions. If possible, do this when babies and children are sleeping or otherwise occupied and when any unsupportive family members aren't around.

First, you'll work through your checklist on the items you marked as "easy." Then go back and do the items you marked "hard."

Have your kitchen wishlist / shopping list handy to jot down notes. Look for opportunities to organize and rearrange along the way. This isn't the time for a major kitchen reorganization, but you can put to work the organizing principles you read above as you go.

See the notes below for each category. Gather your supplies. If you need it, set the timer. Don't forget to check off the box on the *"Milestones Grid"* when you've spent at least an hour decluttering the kitchen.

1. Pantry

The pantry is probably a large category, but it should be one of the easiest. Why? It's easier to discard food than it is other things. You'll find plenty to throw out in this category. Empty your pantry or the cupboards where you store your food. If necessary, do this one shelf at a time.

Throw out: anything you don't like, that your family won't touch, or that has gone stale. Odds and ends collect in the pantry, and we often forget about them. If you find something you're not sure about, ask yourself if you can put it on the menu THIS week. If not, be honest with yourself and let it go.

Why you're not losing money by throwing away food:
People often feel that it's wasteful to throw away uneaten food. While I'm not going to encourage you to be wasteful, let's put it into another light. If you've bought food that no one is going to eat, ***the waste has already occurred***. You're not going to make it worse by throwing it out. ***That money is gone***! So either put it on the menu or toss it, and promise yourself not to buy it again in the future.

Let me tell you what's more wasteful than throwing away some cans and half-used boxes of food: wasting your cupboard space by storing things no one will eat, or wasting your counter space because the cupboards are too full to hold anything else.

How about donating to a food pantry?
This is a good option for jars, cans, and fairly new, unopened boxes of food. If you have a lot of this food, you can set aside a box for donations. But do not let this noble desire interfere with your progress. Better to throw it out if you can't make it to the food pantry than to have it sit in the pantry for many more months (and please don't throw tomatoes at me for saying so!).

Wipe out the dust and crumbs from each shelf after you've decluttered its contents. Make a note on your shopping list of any containers you would like to get to keep the pantry neater. Move on to the next shelf.

2. Pots and pans

Do you have more pots and pans than you need? Are there any that are scratched or in bad condition? Are there lids that don't match anything? Throw 'em out. Are there certain ones that you hate to cook with? Do you have duplicates of the same size that you don't need? Put them into your donate basket.

Pots and pans take up tons of space. Each one must earn its place in your cupboards. This is an area where it pays to invest in quality. I've been using my set of Farberware stainless steel cookware for 20 years! Cast iron skillets will last generations!

3. Junk drawer

Every kitchen has one, maybe several. We all need a place to drop odds and ends, but if you're decluttering, then junk really should go! Empty out your junk drawer. Here are some easy candidates to declutter:

- rubber bands (how many do you really need?)
- coins (put them in your wallet or give them to your kids)
- broken pens and crayons and pencil stubs
- anything that belongs somewhere else (Legos, toys, tools, etc.)
- extra pairs of scissors

Does your junk drawer hold things that no one can identify? These mystery items can sit in junk drawers for years. If you're concerned about these things being important, put them aside and ask everyone in the family about them. If no one knows, you are probably safe throwing them out.

How about stray keys? I hate to throw out stray keys. What if it's important and I don't have it when I need it? My solution for keys is to try to find out what it belongs to and label it immediately. I have a little bucket full of extra keys in the kitchen to keep them together and out of the junk drawer. But I always try to label any new keys that come into the house ASAP.

If your junk drawers don't have any dividers, you might want to add that to your shopping list, or grab some little containers from elsewhere in the house. After you have decluttered what you can and added dividers, the junk drawer will look much better. You'll be able to find things more easily, too.

4. Cleaning supplies and kitchen linens

Cleaning supplies can multiply, can't they? It's important to separate cleaning supplies from food and also to keep them out of reach of small children. Go through your stash, culling out the empty bottles and things you never use. Toss all those yucky sponges and scrubbers. Make notes of things that are running out. Do you need a caddy to corral them all together?

If you use cloth rags for cleaning, sort through these, too. If you have more than you need, toss the ones in the worst condition. Sort kitchen towels and washcloths, too. Do you need to put new towels on your shopping list?

5. Food storage containers

When you sort storage containers, first match up all your lids and bottoms. Any extra lids can go right in the trash. Also, any containers that are cracked, damaged or stained can be discarded. If you've got more containers than you need, pick your favorites and add the rest to the trash or the donate box.

Since you're decluttering the kitchen, now is a great time to treat yourself to some new containers. They don't cost a lot and you can consolidate storage space by getting identical containers in just a few sizes that either nest together when empty (plastic) or that stack neatly (glass).

6. Serving dishes

Since serving dishes (large bowls, platters, casserole dishes, etc.) don't wear out like linens or plasticware, they can stick around practically forever. Collect all your serving dishes in one spot and assess. Do you have some that are difficult to store? Do you do less entertaining than you used to? Is anything chipped? If your family is growing, maybe you need to put a few serving dishes on your shopping list. Take this opportunity to declutter all the dishes you no longer need or want. Your kitchen cupboards will thank you, and you'll be glad not to store all that unwanted clutter any more.

7. Dishes and cutlery

Do you have multiple sets of dishes? Good china and everyday dishes, perhaps? If something in this category is quite sentimental for you, you'll want to leave that portion for later. Bring all your dishes out into the open and decide if there's anything that needs to go or to be replaced. Do the same for all the silverware.

8. Small appliances

Oh, the promises of small appliances! Blenders, mixers, crock pots, juicers, grills, etc. Think of all the things you can make if you just have the proper tool! I am a big fan of having good tools. I use my food processor practically every day. However, I do know that the lure doesn't always play out the way we expect. Sometimes you try something out and the result is meh. Or it stops working and you haven't bothered to get it fixed. You bury it in the back of the cupboard.

Take a deep breath and pull out all your small appliances. Assess them all together. Do you use that crockpot? Is that blender doing what it promised? Do you like the waffle iron? If the answer is an enthusiastic yes, then you've got a keeper. If not, set that one aside to declutter. If it was fairly expensive and it's relatively new, you might be able to sell it and recoup some money. Or bless a friend who may be thrilled to accept it. Or bless a stranger at the thrift store. Decluttering small appliances frees up major cupboard space.

9. Gadgets and tools

Gadgets and tools are similar to appliances, but they take up less space. However, you may have many more of them. Some people LOVE kitchen gadgets. My mother has exactly the right tool for each cooking need. She has a spot for everything and she's content with her selection. I, on the hand, have many fewer than she does. I don't like keeping a tool I'll only use a couple times a year. So I'll choose the next best thing out of my drawer. Both of us are happy with our selections and neither of us is more right than the other.

Collect and assess your selection of kitchen tools and gadgets. Certainly, with your focus on decluttering, you'll find plenty that you don't want to spend the storage space on. Declutter away and remember not to let how much you paid influence your decision.

10. Paperwork

Paperwork is a bit different and could probably occupy its own book! But paperwork needs to be mentioned here because the kitchen is often its holding ground.

Here's my paperwork management system in brief:

- Cancel all the mail you can. All those catalogs that come in the mail that you don't want – spend 30 seconds calling the customer service number to cancel when you get one in the mail.

- Open all the mail each day. Recycle the envelopes. Recycle any junk mail immediately. Don't let it pile up!

- Get each adult in the house an inbox or basket. Put their mail in their inbox. They sort and manage their own mail.

- Have a system to manage bills. This can be as simple as clipping them together and keeping them in your inbox until you're ready to pay them.

- Sort through your inbox once a week.

- Have a basket or shelf just for school papers. Recycle as much school paperwork as you can every day. Anything that you keep, either short term or long term, goes on that dedicated spot for school papers. If you need something, you can quickly sort through the pile. When the pile gets too big, sort the whole thing again, recycle most of it and keep the important papers or your child's best work.

- Have a long term filing system for important papers.

11. Fridge / freezer

I left this until the end of the list, not because it's emotionally draining, but because it can be a big job. Decluttering the fridge and freezer requires a good bit of cleaning. Take things out, one or two shelves at a time. Put the shelves and door compartments into a sink full of soapy water and give them a good washing. See how many condiments you can toss.

In our house, several of the kids are hot sauce lovers so we have a tremendous collection of hot sauces! Some of them are favorites and some not so much. This is one item I'll declutter quickly with those kids. I have no idea which sauces they like. They have no problem telling me to toss the ones that don't make the cut.

Toss any gross leftovers. Even if something isn't spoiled, sometimes you need to let it go. If no one has eaten it yet, what are the odds that it will get consumed? Clutter lives in the fridge, too.

Wipe down the inside of the fridge and put everything back.

Makes notes on your menu if there is food you want to use up quickly.

12. Other

What else do you have in your kitchen? A large cookbook collection? Special wine glasses? A bunch of paper goods? Try to categorize whatever is left and declutter it a category at a time.

Breathe a sigh of relief!

The kitchen was a huge area to declutter! Whether you needed a couple hours or a couple days to declutter your kitchen, I hope you're loving the result! You've worked hard and you deserve to celebrate. Less stuff in your cupboards, in your fridge, and on the counters gives you room to breathe!

Section 4
Build Momentum

The messy middle

There's no doubt about it - you've hit it. You've had an initial burst of energy. Decluttering is fun! Look at how great this is! But then reality sets in. Decluttering is hard. The messes are still coming. Maybe you've gotten rid of a LOT of stuff and you still feel like you haven't made a dent.

It's the "messy middle."

It happens with every project, friend. The initial adrenaline wears off and you're left with just work. It happened to me in the middle of writing this book. I found every excuse imaginable not to keep going. I thought I might play with the dog and check Facebook (as if THAT was a good use of my time!). I suddenly decided to write other articles instead of pressing on toward my deadline.

Don't be discouraged!

The messy middle is not fun. It's the long climb in between the start of the journey and the top of the mountain. And the only way to the top is to push through.

This is why we did all that work in the beginning. Revisit your worksheets. Remind yourself what you're working for. And realize that this apathy, this lack of interest, is normal! It's perfectly reasonable and expected for big projects like this one.

So put on some music! Drink some coffee. Make sure you're cleaning up one space before starting the next one. Pace yourself. Give something away and bless someone else (and check off that box!) It's going to be ok.

I forged through the messy middle. I reminded myself that this happens to me with every project I do. So I sat down and kept writing. And I want you to pick up your plan and choose your next area.

You'll be so glad you did.

Dealing with relatives

Remember how we discussed not decluttering around relatives who will sabotage your progress? Now we're going to talk about how to manage those more difficult relatives.

Some people aren't going to understand your wish to declutter your home. They'll say things like, "Don't be so uptight" and "Oh, but so-and-so gave that to you." They'll bring you things you didn't ask for and that you don't want. They'll try to make you feel guilty for not being "grateful."

This is tough.

If this is an issue for you, here are some things I want you to know. Just like we have decluttering rules, we also have **boundary rules**.

Here they are:

- No one else should make you feel guilty for your own feelings. Creating a guilt trip is not a loving action.

- No one outside your home should dictate what you do or don't keep.

- You are free to keep or dispose of gifts however you please. You are not obligated to keep gifts given to you or your children, no matter how expensive or thoughtful the gift giver was being.

- No one outside your home should decide if you have "enough room" to keep something.

- You do not have to be a storage facility for other people's belongings. Don't allow them to avoid their own issues with clutter by storing it at your house.

- You can say no with love and still remain firm.

Here's how this plays out.

Situation A – Someone often brings over unsolicited gifts for your child.

What to do:
Take this person aside and tell them lovingly and firmly that your child has enough toys / clothes / etc. and ask that they please stop bringing more into your home. Tell them if they continue to bring gifts, you may need to pass these gifts on to people who can better use them.

The next time a gift arrives, thank the giver. When he or she has left, put the gift away and donate it as soon as possible. No explanation required. If the giver questions you about the gift, you remind them of your earlier conversation and that you found a better home for it. Feel free to blame your actions on that decluttering book you read. Then change the subject.

Situation B – An unwanted family heirloom

You've had a large family heirloom in your home for many years. You've never liked it but now that you're decluttering you realize how much you really don't care for it. You gingerly mention to a relative that you are considering replacing it with something new and more suitable to your décor. The relative reacts angrily and questions your dedication to family and your love for the previous owner of the heirloom.

What to do:
Deep breath. Keeping or decluttering an object doesn't define how much you love someone. It sounds like this relative is trying to foist her own guilt off on you. You can offer the heirloom to her or offer it to other family members. There are several suggestions in the next section on dealing with sentimental clutter. But whatever you decide to do, don't allow someone else to bully you into keeping something you don't care for. Have someone else present for moral support if you do end up decluttering this item.

Specifics for clothing, books, and crafts

Here are some tips on decluttering a few more categories.

Decluttering Clothing

There are so many reasons people hang on to clothing – you may have worn different sizes before and after having a baby. You may still be hanging on to "someday" clothes for when you lose a few pounds (I'm guilty on this count). Maybe you have t-shirts that bring back fond memories from college. Or maybe you have expensive clothes in your closet, so you think you need to keep them even though you don't care for a lot of them.

When you're ready to declutter your clothes, go back to the same framework:

- Identify what area to declutter

- Set the timer

- Collect your items

- Sort / take notes

- Dispose of the clutter

- Clean everything up

If clothing is overwhelming, you can do 20-minute sessions with one sub-category at a time: tops, jeans, t-shirts, socks, etc.

When I decluttered my clothing, I thought I wouldn't find much to discard. I decluttered this area with a professional stylist and friend of mine who helped me evaluate my wardrobe. My wardrobe isn't at all large by typical standards. I thought my closet was spartan. But taking every item out and sorting things made me realize all the things I was keeping that I didn't at all like. I had an entire drawer full of jeans that didn't fit and way too many t-shirts that were in poor condition.

The interesting thing was we also found plenty of things that I wasn't wearing that look great on me! Since there were so many things I didn't like, it was hard to notice some of the more flattering clothes when I got dressed each day.

My discard pile was enormous once we were done. We kept a shopping list of wardrobe classics to round out my wardrobe. Then my friend went shopping with me and helped me find things that flattered my body.

What if I have nothing left to wear?!

I was really concerned with this possibility when I decluttered my clothing.

This may be true, but likely you'll still have plenty, even if you're down to a small selection. You may need to go shopping.

What's more likely is that you've only been rotating through a very small portion of your clothes and ignoring the rest. When you get rid of the wardrobe clutter, you can see what you've got and it's so much more enjoyable to get dressed. I had fallen into the trap of wearing unflattering and boring clothes. Now I enjoy looking nicer with clothes that flatter and fit. I only saved a few older things to use for yard work and dirty jobs.

When you declutter your clothes, you'll also:

- have less laundry to do

- be able to keep your closet neater

- feel better about yourself because you're wearing things you love

You can read the full story of how I decluttered my closet and find some laundry tips to keep your clothing in great shape on my blog here: ***http://www.declutteringschool.com/declutter-your-closet/***

What if you can't afford to buy a whole new wardrobe?

Again, you may be wearing the same few items over and over again. Decluttering the rest won't change that – you'll just be able to see what you're actually wearing. Plus, as with all decluttering, if you stop spending money on clothing you don't love, and especially avoid buying things just because they're a good deal, you'll find you're able to invest in better quality clothing. I now enjoy a small wardrobe with high-quality, classic pieces. These clothes fit better and last longer than cheaper items.

Another one of my clothing tips is to shop at thredUP.com. ThredUP is an online consignment store with high quality clothing including plenty of designer brands. They have free returns, so if you don't love something, you can send it right back without buyer's remorse and without the hassle of an extra trip to the store.

You can also make a few bucks by sending them your unneeded clothing clutter, although they are fairly picky about what brands they accept. ThredUP has clothing for women and children.

Decluttering books

Some people consider books to be a sacred category. You might be willing to declutter lots of different things but never even consider parting with a book. After all, books are good, right? You want your kids to love reading, especially if you're a reader yourself. But books can be clutter, too, my friends. I had books on my shelves I NEVER EVEN READ! That's not smart or studious, although maybe it looks that way to visitors in your home.

Unfortunately, keeping books you don't value is as wasteful of money and storage space as any other clutter.

When decluttering books, as with all your other categories, start with the easy ones. I'll bet when you start looking at your bookshelves, you'll find books you never liked. Books that are falling apart (first editions excepted). Technical books get out of date very quickly. That programming manual or college test prep book from 1998 is probably useless. Unfortunately, books like these belong in the trash.

If you're keeping books from a former period of your life, it may be hard to let these go. I felt like this about my gardening books. I had quite a collection, but I don't garden much now. I've moved on to other hobbies.

After keeping an entire shelf of gardening books through a move and for much too long, I finally decluttered. I cut back to my two favorites and the rest went to the library book sale. I'm sure someone was pleased to find them. Hopefully they're inspiring beautiful new gardens for other people.

Owning gardening books didn't make me a gardener. Now I don't feel like I *should* be gardening when I look at that shelf. If I decide to spend some time working in my garden (which I still do from time to time), I will do it without obligation. And there's plenty of garden advice and inspiration on Pinterest or in a new book if I need it.

Decluttering and children

There are two kinds of decluttering where children are concerned:

- Decluttering while your kids are **nearby** or underfoot

- Decluttering with your kids **actively involved** and helping to make decisions

The first type may tax your patience. If your kids are little or high maintenance, you'll probably have to stick to 20-minute sessions (or less!) Tell your kids what's going on, show them your timer and let them know you'll do something with them when you're done.

Your kids are watching you all the time! Use the opportunity to reinforce some positive attitudes about "stuff" and the work it takes to declutter. Show them how rewarding this work is for you. Help them see the satisfaction of a job well done. Staying cheerful will also help you get through the work without burning out.

As you talk to your kids, plant seeds in their minds about all the wonderful things you're looking forward to as you declutter.

Say things like:

"It'll be so quick to clean up the kitchen when we're done – we'll be able to start our family movie night earlier!"

"Now that we've gotten rid of all this clutter, we can see all our favorite books on the shelf."

"I can tell this is your favorite toy because you always put it on the shelf so nicely when you're done."

You want them to develop positive attitudes toward cleaning up and decluttering. If they think you are miserable during this time and that you dread decluttering, they'll feel the same way about maintaining their own possessions. So model a good attitude and keep it upbeat.

If your kids are willing helpers, you can put them to work carrying things back and forth. Toddlers and even older kids may feel very important doing "heavy" lifting like this and it will keep them out of trouble.

**You can also declutter WITH your kids.
I do it all the time with my own kids.**

I was decluttering toys the other day with my youngest son who is four years old. By now, he's a decluttering pro. I asked him if he wanted to keep a certain puzzle. His answer? "I don't want it anymore, but first I want to do it one more time." How's that for a mature attitude about letting go?!

This boy, he's not naturally a minimalist. He's had tons of practice decluttering and tidying up his toys with me. We use the same decluttering framework I laid out in Section 2.

When you declutter with your child, keep things focused and as brief as possible. Kids aren't capable of working for hours at a time on a project like this. Pick a narrow category. Start with "puzzles" or "baby toys" or some other focused area. As your child handles each item, discuss the standard decluttering questions with her: Do you love this item? Do you still use it? Do we have room to keep it? Is it in good condition?

Make sure your child knows it's his decision to keep or declutter something. If you plan to get rid of something regardless of his opinion, then make that clear upfront and possibly make that a separate session. Be willing to accept that she might *not* love some of the toys that you do. He may decide to keep certain things you consider junk. My kids frequently surprise me with what they do and don't want to keep.

Decluttering toys shouldn't take lots of time.

If you follow the framework and make quick decisions, you can go through an entire box or shelf of toys in 15 minutes or less.

What if my child wants to hold on to every last gum wrapper and broken matchbox car? Maybe he needs to see you modeling some good decluttering behavior before he's ready to attempt it himself. And by all means, feel free to declutter when your child is not home if you feel that's the right option for your family. Parents do have the authority to make these kinds of decisions for their kids. If you do this, expect some drama from your kid, but it won't last terribly long.

How many toys are too many?

This question will depend on how much storage space you have and how much patience you have for cleaning up (and hopefully your kids do most of the clean-up). I've never aimed for a certain number of toys; instead, we just try to keep what we love and ditch the rest. And we encourage non-gift toys for birthdays and Christmas to keep the clutter from returning.

Of course, new toys do find their way into the house. Plus, kids eventually outgrow their favorites. So you're likely going to have to declutter periodically. If you have a nostalgic attachment to some toys like baby items and toys from your own childhood, you might need extra motivation to go through those things.

Not all my kids are so enthusiastic about decluttering as my four-year-old. But they all know the drill. We recently decluttered hoodies. How on earth can one family have so many hoodies? I have no idea, but now we have half as many as when we started.

Section 5
You're Becoming a Pro!

Dealing with Sentimental Items

Can I tell you a secret? Maybe you've already discovered this, but decluttering isn't really about the stuff. Decluttering is about emotions. Guilt, uncertainty, sadness, fear. And all these emotions come to a head when you're faced with physical things that stir up these feelings for you. You can choose to hang on to the things and keep bearing the weight of the emotions or you can choose to let go of the things and face an even greater emotional toll. At least that's what your feelings are likely telling you.

But here's the thing about these feelings – the guilt, the sadness, the regret – as long as you allow them to influence your life, you'll never be free of them. Be willing to take action about these feelings, on the other hand and there's a huge shift. While you may have a temporary surge in feelings of guilt, sadness, etc., it's usually much briefer than you anticipated. The relief that follows is immense. After all, no one wants to walk around continually reminded of some source of guilt or regret. You don't deserve that in your life!

This is a long way to say that the clutter you're leaving until last – those sentimental items – they're putting a burden on you that you don't have to carry. Holding on to those things, if all they bring you is guilt or fear, is only dragging you down. At the beginning of this decluttering process, we talked about the need to be honest with yourself about what things you truly love and use. Now this need is even greater, more urgent. Only you can know if something is clutter or cherished. And if you decide it's clutter, then the sooner you are rid of it the better!

Hopefully I've convinced you of this need. But what do you DO with these things now? The thought of putting them in the trash is probably too painful to bear. I hear you. Instead of that, let's see if any of these choices sound more appealing.

Here are some suggestions to help you release sentimental items.

Put out an open invite to your relatives.

If you have things from people who have passed away or who are no longer able to keep them, a great choice is to say something like this:

"We are re-arranging the house a bit and we no longer have room for XYZ. Would anyone like to have it?"

You don't have to elaborate why you don't have room – just put it like that and people will be more likely to accept your reasons. Maybe someone else will be thrilled to have that heirloom tea set or the portrait of your ancestor.

Give to a friend.

You may be hanging on to something that you no longer need or want. Put up a note on Facebook asking if anyone could use this thing. You might be surprised who would be thrilled to have what you're offering.

Find a worthy cause.

Some things are hard to get rid of, not because of their historical value, but because you have such an emotional attachment to them. It was like this with homeschool books for me. I ended up gifting them to another homeschool family who was thrilled to have them. It was easier for me to do this rather than just donate the books to the library book sale. I knew they would be appreciated. Other worthy causes that might welcome your donations: Daycare centers, historical societies, women's or homeless shelters, foster care agencies, animal shelters. You can find places that repurpose old wedding gowns into teddy bears for needy children. Get creative and you may end up being thrilled with the new life your item receives.

Take a picture.

Sometimes it's as easy as taking a picture and then donating or giving away the item.

Sell it and donate the proceeds.

Perhaps you have an old set of silver that you really don't care for. Maybe you can sell it and donate the money to a cause in honor of the person it reminds you of.

Keep one and dispose of the rest.

With a selection of items (school papers, baby clothes, etc.) that you can't bring yourself to part with, you may be satisfied with keeping your absolute favorite item and decluttering the others.

Ask someone else to donate or dispose of it for you.

Perhaps you can't bear the thought of getting rid of something, but you can ask someone else to do it while you're not home.

Write up your memories.

If you're dealing with things like children's school papers or artwork, you might find enjoyment in leafing through them and writing a letter of what thoughts those papers evoke.

Repurpose.

If you're creative or crafty, you may enjoy turning your older item into something new and different (baby clothes become a quilt, make artwork into a photo book). Just remember to be honest with yourself and don't plan to do this kind of a project unless you really want to, and you honestly know you'll find the time to do it. You don't want to create more opportunities to procrastinate.

Mourn.

Some things may evoke such painful feelings that you need to allow yourself to mourn. Maybe you've been holding onto something to avoid dealing with the pain of loss. Acknowledge your feelings. Spend some time with your memories and you may find it easier or at least possible to part with the thing that's causing you grief.

Some of these choices are quick and others are a lot more work. Take your time deciding and be kind to yourself.

Three tips to maintaining your spaces and staying organized

Are you excited to be at this point in your decluttering journey? Even if you've only done a few decluttering sessions, you're miles ahead of where you were when you started. Your hard work is paying off! Now that you've worked so hard, you don't want all that effort to be undone by filling up with clutter all over again.

Here are some tips to help you maintain your newly uncluttered spaces.

1. Finish what you started.

A lot of the clutter in our homes is just stuff that needs to be put away. It's easy to leave a coffee cup on the counter (just til later). Or to do a craft project and leave the materials out when you're done. But that coffee cup turns into stacks of dirty dishes. And those craft supplies start to cover the table.

These are all jobs that got started and never finished.

Here's how to avoid this problem.

If you get something to eat, make sure the dishes are 100% cleaned up when you're done.

If you do a project, you're not done until everything is cleaned up.

If your kids come home from school, they should be taking care of their shoes, backpacks, lunchboxes, etc. immediately.

Otherwise, these things have to be done later. And we all know that later doesn't show up very willingly. Do it right away and it hardly seems like an extra job at all!

If you train yourself (and your family) to finish what you start, you'll have so much less clutter to manage! It's truly life-changing!

2. Your mindset is critical!

Remember all that work you did upfront to evaluate what clutter is costing you? Use your new skills to make sure you don't go back to that place. You don't want to be overwhelmed by the clutter and the mess. You *want* to enjoy that clean and clear kitchen every day (in between meals, of course). You *want* to have more time to spend on your priorities. You *don't want* that guilt to creep back into your mind.

So be ruthless about keeping on top of clutter! If you catch yourself thinking you'll hold on to something "just in case," stop immediately and ask yourself if it's worth the storage space it will take. If your kids start leaving their things lying around, make sure you're reinforcing a pickup time every day.

3. Empty spaces don't need to be filled.

You may have felt the need in the past to fill up every shelf, every cupboard. You may have viewed a blank space or an empty shelf as an invitation to put something there. Resist that urge. Allow your shelves, cupboards and drawers some breathing room. You may even end up with empty drawers!

You will likely find things to put in those spaces eventually. It happens naturally. But don't view an empty space as something that needs filling.

This is a great time to share some before and after pics of your hard work! Post your pictures on Facebook or Instagram. This is a great way to enjoy your progress. Make sure to check off the box on the "*Milestones Grid*" when you do this.

Three questions to ask before buying new things

Once you've spent some time decluttering, you'll find that you feel differently about buying new things. After getting rid of all that stuff, you're not going to want to fill it up again with more stuff that you end up decluttering later. So it's helpful to get in the habits of being more intentional with your purchases. Here are three questions to ask yourself before making a purchase.

1. Is this something I love or is it just a "good deal" that I'm going to regret later?

I love a good deal as much as the next person! I used to love scouring clothing stores for sales. I'd come home with a bag full of marked down bargains. The problem was those clothes often didn't fit well. Even if it was only a few bucks, now I had clothing I didn't love cluttering up my closet. Ugh. The same can happen in the kitchen aisle or even the dollar store.

I still shop around for deals, but I don't buy things unless I absolutely love them. It's just not worth it in terms of money or clutter.

2. Do I have a place for it? Does something else need to be decluttered if I buy this?

This is hard!! Don't bring things into your home if storage is tight. Are you willing to give up something in order to get something else? If the answer is no, perhaps this is a purchase you should skip.

3. Do I have something else that already fills this need?

Just because there's the perfect tool to do something doesn't mean you need to get it. How many kitchen tools do I have that do the same thing? Be careful with your purchases and see if you can't make do with an item you already own. You'll avoid extra clutter AND save money too!

A suggested decluttering order

In general, you should declutter your areas from easiest to hardest with the exception of putting the kitchen close to the beginning.

Here's how I prioritize deciding what to declutter and when:

- Easy areas / getting into a decluttering mindset
- The kitchen. Get the heart of your home whipped into shape.
- Other "easy-ish" areas
- Harder areas
- Hardest areas to face

What you choose to declutter and when will vary greatly depending on what's easiest for you. You may have no issue with toys, but the thought of decluttering your closet causes great anxiety. Or maybe your kitchen is in great shape, but the basement is a mess. Take this list and rearrange it into the best order for you. The process will get much easier as you go.

More details on picking the order that's right for you

1. 20-minute decluttering sessions

As many as possible to clear up focused problem areas. Pick the ones you're most motivated to do. Keep notes about things you want to buy to make these areas easier to maintain.

- Incoming mail
- Junk drawer
- Individual bookshelves (one at a time)
- Coats and jackets
- Shoes
- Your purse
- Under the bathroom sinks
- Cleaning supplies
- Laundry supplies
- Pet supplies

Give yourself some quick wins at the beginning to gain momentum.

2. Conquer the kitchen.

Make a big impact and save yourself plenty of time once you're done with this area.

3. Areas of medium difficulty

- Display cabinets and shelves (knick-knacks, picture frames, etc.)
- Toys
- Closets / clothing – yours
- Closets / clothing – children's

4. Areas of maximum difficulty
(suggestions only - yours may be different)

- Books
- Paperwork
- Garage
- Basement and other storage spaces
- Other sentimental items you've left until last

It may take you many months or even years to work through all your things. That's ok! It's not a race. Plus, you'll get the biggest return by tackling your key problem areas and creating some easy wins for yourself. If it takes you several years to get to the box of family photos, don't sweat it. I won't tell!

Work through at least two more decluttering sessions and check off those boxes on the "*Milestones Grid!*"

Time to Reflect

Once you've made it through the *Milestones Grid,* take some time to look back on your journey. Did it work out the way you expected? Was it as hard as you feared? Reflecting on your progress right now will help you keep moving forward and avoid reverting back to previous bad habits.

ACTION ITEM

Fill out the "*Personal Reflection*" Worksheet.

Conclusion

I hope this book has given you a new outlook on the clutter in your home. I hope you've come away encouraged. Making a change like this doesn't happen overnight. You've got to deal with emotions, relationships and a lot of stuff! It takes time and it can be mentally exhausting. But the rewards are tremendous! You can do it!

The Decluttering School Roadmap

Congratulations! You've just completed Step-by-Step Decluttering. If you ordered the complete digital Step-by-Step Decluttering Workshop, make sure you've logged into our website. You have access to many bonus trainings and resources there. If you would like to purchase, you can do so at

https://declutteringschool.com/shop/

Where do you go from here?

Step-by-Step Decluttering has given you the foundation for decluttering your home so that it's a space you can feel proud of. Now you're invited to continue your journey toward becoming even more organized so that life gets easier and you have more time and energy for the things that matter most.

After Step-by-Step Decluttering, we recommend you pick the area that you'd like to work on next:

- **Household Paperwork Made Easy**: Conquer all your paper piles and say goodbye to paperwork anxiety

- **Organize My Home membership**: Get support from our decluttering community with numerous live group calls every week and over 100 decluttering and organizing trainings and counting

- **Organize Like a Boss challenge**: Declutter and organize 5 hotspots in your home with our live class

All these products and more are available in our shop at **https://declutteringschool.com/shop/**

Please direct any questions about your purchases to our Customer Success team at **sarah@declutteringschool.com**.

About the Author

Sarah Mueller is the creator of Decluttering School, formerly known as Early Bird Mom, mom to four of the most rambunctious boys you will ever meet.

Upbeat encourager of overwhelmed women, Sarah Mueller founded and authors the blog Decluttering School, which offers guidance on decluttering and organizing. Sarah also created two highly-popular Facebook communities, Decluttering Club and Declutter My Home, where she motivates members to pare down and tidy up. Facebook recently recruited Mueller to help them pilot their new Subscription Groups program with her new brainchild, Organize My Home, a targeted training group that gives tools to organize and clean cluttered spaces.

Connect with Sarah:

Web: https://www.declutteringschool.com

Facebook: https://www.facebook.com/EarlybirdMom

Pinterest: https://www.pinterest.com/sarahsmueller/

Instagram: @declutteringclub

Email: sarah@declutteringschool.com

STEP
- BY -
STEP
DECLUTTERING
WORKSHEETS

SARAH MUELLER

Decluttering Milestones Grid

Decluttering is hard work but so rewarding! I want you to get motivated and inspired as you work through this book! Use this grid to keep track of your progress and celebrate your milestones. Cross off each box as you go.

Print all worksheets and put on a clipboard or in a folder	**Complete the *You are Here* and *Cost of Clutter* Worksheets**	**Complete the *Donate / Sell / Trash* Worksheet**
Do a 20 minute decluttering session If there's time, do another session.	**Complete the Decluttering the *Kitchen Checklist***	**Spend 1 hour decluttering your kitchen**
Give something away	**Take a load of things in good condition to the thrift store.**	**Do another 1 hour decluttering session**
Share before and after pictures on Facebook, Pinterest or Instagram with #stepbystepdecluttering	**Do another 1 hour decluttering session**	**Complete the *Personal Reflection* Worksheet**

STEP-BY-STEP DECLUTTERING   WORKSHEET

Worksheet: You are Here

Today's date:	
What area do you most want to declutter?	
Imagine - write 3 words that describe how you'd love this area to look when you're done.	
What things do you expect to be pretty easy to declutter?	
What are you dreading the most? Does this area or these things absolutely have to be decluttered? (I recommend leaving the harder stuff for later.)	
What things make it more difficult for you to declutter: Ex.: Health issues, volume of clutter, small children, family members, busy schedule	
Any upcoming deadlines for decluttering: Ex.: New baby, moving house, big party, etc.	
When do you have time to declutter over the next 2 weeks? Be realistic but also as aggressive as possible with your times. Ex.: After dinner, on Saturday from 1-3pm, while the kids are at school, 30 minutes each afternoon	
What can you do to get help with this process? Ex.: Someone to do some heavy lifting? Moral support from a friend? Someone to take the kids for an afternoon? Work together with spouse?	
Who can be your cheerleader during this process?	
Who is less likely to be supportive?	
What can you do to make this process more enjoyable? (Suggestions: take before and after photos, play music, look forward to a small reward at the end, post about progress on Facebook, etc.)	

STEP-BY-STEP DECLUTTERING   WORKSHEET

Clutter: Cost / Benefit

Check off the items that apply to you.

Cost of Clutter: What do you want to eliminate?	Benefits of Decluttering: What are you looking forward to?
☐ Frustration	☐ Your treasures are enjoyed
☐ Time spent looking for things	☐ Pleasant and enjoyable spaces
☐ Depression	☐ Easy to clean
☐ Embarrassment	☐ Enjoyable to work and play in
☐ Live in the past and miss out on the present and possibilities for the future	☐ You can find what you're looking for
☐ Wasted money	☐ Easier to focus on your work or family
☐ Collects dust, visually unappealing	☐ More time for your priorities
☐ Over-stimulating babies and children	☐ Less temptation to buy unnecessary things and destroy your hard work
☐ Negative mindset	☐ Invest in quality purchases (clothing, furniture, etc.) which will last much longer
☐ Dangerous - trip hazards and fire hazards	☐ Incentive to be thoughtful about new purchases
☐ Extra work to maintain and clean	☐ More room to work and play
☐ Hard to motivate yourself to start projects	☐ Teach children good habits for the future
☐ Guilt over unused purchases	☐ Kids will play for longer periods and more peacefully when fewer toys are available
☐ Hides the things you do love	☐ Decluttered homes point towards the future instead of hanging on to the past.
☐ Money spent on storage unit	

STEP-BY-STEP DECLUTTERING   WORKSHEET

Donate / Sell / Trash: What to do with all that stuff

Decide which options you'll utilize for the things you declutter. You may revise these choices as you go, but it's good to have an idea upfront what you're going to with your clutter.

Trash / Recycle ☐ Yes ☐ No ☐ Maybe

Donate ☐ Yes ☐ No ☐ Maybe

Where will you donate?

Ask your friends ☐ Yes ☐ No ☐ Maybe

Do you have any items in mind to offer to friends?

Find a worthy cause ☐ Yes ☐ No ☐ Maybe

Do you have any special items in mind to go to a worthy cause?

Sell ☐ Yes ☐ No ☐ Maybe

Where will you sell?

Do you have anything in mind to sell yet?

Repurpose ☐ Yes ☐ No ☐ Maybe

Do you have anything in mind to repurpose?

STEP-BY-STEP DECLUTTERING   WORKSHEET

Decluttering the Kitchen: Checklist

Some areas of the kitchen will be easier than others. Evaluate how much mental effort you'll need to do each category. There's room for you to write in 3 more sections depending on your needs. Indicate how much emotional effort will you need to declutter the specific area? When you finish a section, check it off with glee!

1. Pantry
☐ **Easy** ☐ **Hard** ☐ **Too difficult - save for later** ☐ **Complete**

2. Pots and pans
☐ **Easy** ☐ **Hard** ☐ **Too difficult - save for later** ☐ **Complete**

3. Junk drawer
☐ **Easy** ☐ **Hard** ☐ **Too difficult - save for later** ☐ **Complete**

4. Cleaning supplies and kitchen linens
☐ **Easy** ☐ **Hard** ☐ **Too difficult - save for later** ☐ **Complete**

5. Food storage containers
☐ **Easy** ☐ **Hard** ☐ **Too difficult - save for later** ☐ **Complete**

6. Serving dishes
☐ **Easy** ☐ **Hard** ☐ **Too difficult - save for later** ☐ **Complete**

7. Dishes and cutlery
☐ **Easy** ☐ **Hard** ☐ **Too difficult - save for later** ☐ **Complete**

8. Small appliances
☐ **Easy** ☐ **Hard** ☐ **Too difficult - save for later** ☐ **Complete**

9. Gadgets and tools
☐ **Easy** ☐ **Hard** ☐ **Too difficult - save for later** ☐ **Complete**

10. Paperwork
☐ **Easy** ☐ **Hard** ☐ **Too difficult - save for later** ☐ **Complete**

11. Fridge / freezer
☐ **Easy** ☐ **Hard** ☐ **Too difficult - save for later** ☐ **Complete**

12.
☐ **Easy** ☐ **Hard** ☐ **Too difficult - save for later** ☐ **Complete**

13.
☐ **Easy** ☐ **Hard** ☐ **Too difficult - save for later** ☐ **Complete**

14.
☐ **Easy** ☐ **Hard** ☐ **Too difficult - save for later** ☐ **Complete**

Kitchen Wishlist / Shopping List

Need to get for the kitchen	Nice to have someday...

STEP-BY-STEP DECLUTTERING   WORKSHEET

Personal Reflection Worksheet

1. One thing I was surprised about decluttering was:

2. The hardest things to declutter were:

3. The easiest things to declutter were:

4. Now that I've made it this far, I feel:

5. One habit I don't want to go back to is:

6. To avoid this old habit, 2 things I'll do are: